KINSEY'S LOG

WHATCOM MUSEUM OF HISTORY AND ART, BELLINGHAM, WASHINGTON
A BOOK OF POSTCARDS • POMEGRANATE ARTBOOKS • SAN FRANCISCO

Pomegranate
Box 6099
Rohnert Park, CA 94927

Pomegranate Europe Ltd.
Fullbridge House, Fullbridge
Maldon, Essex CM9 4LE
England

ISBN 0-87654-905-9
Pomegranate Catalog No. A846

© 1996 D. Kinsey Collection,
Whatcom Museum of History and Art, Bellingham, Washington

Pomegranate publishes books
of postcards on a wide range of subjects.
Please write to the publisher for more information.

Designed by Young Jin Kim
Printed in Korea

07 06 05 04 03 02 01 00 99 98   11 10 9 8 7 6 5 4 3 2

To facilitate detachment of the postcards from this book, fold each card along its perforation line before tearing.

The steam locomotives pictured in this book of postcards were built in the early 1900s in response to the logging industry's changing needs for motive power. As logging operations moved farther uphill in search of standing timber, more efficient locomotives were required to pull the heavy loads up the steeper logging tracks, particularly in the Pacific Northwest. Before the turn of the century, Ephraim Shay, a Michigan logger, developed a radically new geared locomotive that proved highly suitable for the new conditions. The Shay locomotive was soon followed by designs from a number of competing manufacturers, most notably Heisler and Climax, and later by heavier versions of conventional rod-and-piston locomotives, such as those of the Baldwin Locomotive Works.

These thirty remarkable images are part of the life's work of the husband-and-wife photographic team of Darius (1869–1945) and Tabitha (1875–1963) Kinsey, who operated the Timber Views Company in Seattle beginning in 1907. With Darius in the field and Tabitha in the darkroom, the Kinseys created a stunning photographic record of the fascinating era of the steam locomotive in the Pacific Northwest. Today the Kinsey Collection is housed in the Whatcom Museum of History and Art in Bellingham, Washington.

KINSEY'S LOCOMOTIVES

Three-truck Shay (Lima Locomotive Works), Merrill & Ring Lumber Company, Camp No. 1, near Port Angeles, Washington, c. 1930

Pomegranate Box 6099 Rohnert Park CA 94927

13845
© D. Kinsey Collection, Whatcom Museum of History and Art, Bellingham, Washington

KINSEY'S LOCOMOTIVES

Mallet 2-6-6-2 (Baldwin Locomotive Works), Bloedel
Donovan Lumber Mills, Sekiu, near Clallam Bay, western
Olympic Peninsula, c. 1930s

Pomegranate   Box 6099   Rohnert Park, CA 94927

10144H
© D. Kinsey Collection, Whatcom Museum of History and
Art, Bellingham, Washington

KINSEY'S LOCOMOTIVES

Three-truck Shay (Lima Locomotive Works), Wallace Falls Timber Company, Gold Bar, Snohomish County, Washington, c. 1917

Pomegranate Box 6099 Rohnert Park CA 94927

19025
© D. Kinsey Collection, Whatcom Museum of History and Art, Bellingham, Washington

KINSEY'S LOCOMOTIVES

Mikado 2-8-2 (H. K. Porter Company), Monroe Logging Company, Snohomish County, Washington, c. 1920s

Pomegranate Box 6099 Rohnert Park, CA 94927

13107
© D. Kinsey Collection, Whatcom Museum of History and Art, Bellingham, Washington

KINSEY'S LOCOMOTIVES

Mallet 2-6-6-2 T (Baldwin Locomotive Works), Bloedel Donovan Lumber Mills, near Bellingham, Washington, c. 1925

Pomegranate   Box 6099   Rohnert Park, CA 94927

14018
© D. Kinsey Collection, Whatcom Museum of History and Art, Bellingham, Washington

KINSEY'S LOCOMOTIVES

Three-truck class C Climax (Climax Locomotive Works), operating for the Puget Sound Sawmills and Shingle Company, Baker River Canyon, c. 1922

Pomegranate   Box 6099   Rohnert Park CA 94927

10110D
© D. Kinsey Collection, Whatcom Museum of History and Art, Bellingham, Washington

KINSEY'S LOCOMOTIVES

Shay locomotive (Lima Locomotive Works), English Lumber Company, Conway, Washington, c. 1930

Pomegranate Box 6099 Rohnert Park, CA 94927

13589
© D. Kinsey Collection, Whatcom Museum of History and Art, Bellingham, Washington

KINSEY'S LOCOMOTIVES

Two-truck locomotive (Heisler Locomotive Works), Miller Logging Company, Sultan, Washington, c. 1922

Pomegranate Box 6099 Rohnert Park, CA 94927

13720/34
© D. Kinsey Collection, Whatcom Museum of History and Art, Bellingham, Washington

KINSEY'S LOCOMOTIVES

Two-truck locomotive (Heisler Locomotive Works), Nelson-Neal Lumber Company, Lindwood Camp, near Bryant, Washington, c. 1911

Pomegranate Box 6099 Rohnert Park, CA 94927

20574
© D. Kinsey Collection, Whatcom Museum of History and Art, Bellingham, Washington

KINSEY'S LOCOMOTIVES

Side-tank 2-6-2 (H. K. Porter Company), Charles R. McCormick Lumber Company, Olympic Peninsula near Hood Canal, c. 1928

Pomegranate Box 6099 Rohnert Park CA 94927

14247
© D. Kinsey Collection, Whatcom Museum of History and Art, Bellingham, Washington

KINSEY'S LOCOMOTIVES

Three-truck Shay (Lima Locomotive Works), Hama Hama Logging Company, Olympic Peninsula near Hama Hama River, c. 1925

Pomegranate Box 6099 Rohnert Park CA 94927

14037
© D. Kinsey Collection, Whatcom Museum of History and Art, Bellingham, Washington

KINSEY'S LOCOMOTIVES

2-6-6-2 T (Baldwin Locomotive Works), Bloedel Donovan
Lumber Mills, Clallam County, Washington, c. 1928

Pomegranate Box 6099 Rohnert Park CA 94927

13857/33
© D. Kinsey Collection, Whatcom Museum of History and
Art, Bellingham, Washington

KINSEY'S LOCOMOTIVES

Three-truck Willamette geared locomotive (Shay type) (Willamette Iron & Steel Works), Sauk River Lumber Company, Darrington, Washington, c. 1925

Pomegranate Box 6099 Rohnert Park, CA 94927

13468
© D. Kinsey Collection, Whatcom Museum of History and Art, Bellingham, Washington

KINSEY'S LOCOMOTIVES

Three-truck Shay (Lima Locomotive Works), Sound Timber Company, Darrington, Washington, 1936

Pomegranate   Box 6099   Rohnert Park, CA 94927

14565
© D. Kinsey Collection, Whatcom Museum of History and Art, Bellingham, Washington

KINSEY'S LOCOMOTIVES

Shay locomotive (Lima Locomotive Works), Stimson Timber Company, Belfair, Washington, c. 1924

Pomegranate Box 6099 Rohnert Park CA 94927

14114/94
© D. Kinsey Collection, Whatcom Museum of History and Art, Bellingham, Washington

KINSEY'S LOCOMOTIVES

2-6-6-2 T (Baldwin Locomotive Works), Weyerhaeuser
Timber Company, Vail, Washington, 1938

Pomegranate   Box 6099   Rohnert Park, CA 94927

14804/72
© D. Kinsey Collection, Whatcom Museum of History and
Art, Bellingham, Washington

KINSEY'S LOCOMOTIVES

2-6-6-2 T (Baldwin Locomotive Works), Bloedel Donovan
Lumber Mills, Beaver Camp, Washington, 1925

Pomegranate   Box 6099   Rohnert Park, CA 94927

13044
© D. Kinsey Collection, Whatcom Museum of History and
Art, Bellingham, Washington

KINSEY'S LOCOMOTIVES

Shay locomotive (Lima Locomotive Works), Hama Hama
Logging Company, Hood Canal, Washington, 1928

Pomegranate Box 6099 Rohnert Park, CA 94927

14034
© D. Kinsey Collection, Whatcom Museum of History and
Art, Bellingham, Washington

KINSEY'S LOCOMOTIVES

Two-truck Shay (Lima Locomotive Works), Hama Hama
Logging Company, near Eldon, Hood Canal, Washington,
c. 1926–1930

POMEGRANATE BOX 6099 ROHNERT PARK CA 94927

14046
© D. Kinsey Collection, Whatcom Museum of History and
Art, Bellingham, Washington

KINSEY'S LOCOMOTIVES

Two-truck Shay (Lima Locomotive Works), Monroe
Logging Company, Lake Stevens, Washington, c. 1924

Pomegranate Box 6099 Rohnert Park CA 94927

13733
© D. Kinsey Collection, Whatcom Museum of History and
Art, Bellingham, Washington

KINSEY'S LOCOMOTIVES

Three-truck Shay (Lima Locomotive Works), Charles R. McCormick Lumber Company, Camp Talbot, Quilcene, Washington, 1927

Pomegranate   Box 6099   Rohnert Park CA 94927

13546
© D. Kinsey Collection, Whatcom Museum of History and Art, Bellingham, Washington

KINSEY'S LOCOMOTIVES

Climax locomotive (Climax Manufacturing Company), Webb Logging & Timber Company, McCoy, Washington, 1920

Pomegranate   Box 6099   Rohnert Park, CA 94927

14029
© D. Kinsey Collection, Whatcom Museum of History and Art, Bellingham, Washington

KINSEY'S LOCOMOTIVES

Mikado 2-8-2 (Baldwin Locomotive Works), Siler Logging Company, Duvall, Washington, 1924

Pomegranate Box 6099 Rohnert Park, CA 94927

10144K
© D. Kinsey Collection, Whatcom Museum of History and Art, Bellingham, Washington

KINSEY'S LOCOMOTIVES

Three-truck Shay (Lima Locomotive Works), Clear Lake Lumber Company, Skagit County, Washington, c. 1923

Pomegranate   Box 6099   Rohnert Park, CA 94927

12666
© D. Kinsey Collection, Whatcom Museum of History and Art, Bellingham, Washington

KINSEY'S LOCOMOTIVES

Three-truck Shay (Lima Locomotive Works), Sauk River
Lumber Company, Darrington, Washington, late 1920s

Pomegranate   Box 6099   Rohnert Park, CA 94927

13481
© D. Kinsey Collection, Whatcom Museum of History and
Art, Bellingham, Washington

KINSEY'S LOCOMOTIVES

Two-truck Shay, two-truck Shay, and H. K. Porter Company 0-4-2 T, Stimson Mill Company, Marysville, Washington, c. 1900

Pomegranate Box 6099 Rohnert Park CA 94927

10169
© D. Kinsey Collection, Whatcom Museum of History and Art, Bellingham, Washington

KINSEY'S LOCOMOTIVES

Three-truck locomotive (Climax Manufacturing Company),
Washington Logging Company, Hoodsport, Washington,
c. 1929

Pomegranate Box 6099 Rohnert Park, CA 94927

14049
© D. Kinsey Collection, Whatcom Museum of History and
Art, Bellingham, Washington

KINSEY'S LOCOMOTIVES

Heisler locomotive (rebuilt and regauged by Heisler Locomotive Works), Redmond, Washington, 1922

Pomegranate Box 6099 Rohnert Park, CA 94927

13613
© D. Kinsey Collection, Whatcom Museum of History and Art, Bellingham, Washington